A PERSO
FOR YOU

DEVELOPING COURAGE

Understanding confidence for personal improvement and long-term growth

By Claire & Ralph Moody

Your Free Book Is Waiting

Many people struggle with low confidence and low self-esteem, which affects their professional and personal lives. Your thoughts and feelings have a significant impact and this is where issues can manifest. If we don't do something about it, a lack of confidence will hold you back. This book will give you an opportunity to think about your confidence in a different way.

Get your free copy:

www.jcrm.shop

target
training associates

The authors also own Target Training and the company is recognised as a 5 Star provider by Trustpilot and our testimonials are legendary.

We offer training and coaching services and specialise in Coaching, Training, Management and Personal Development and all our courses can be delivered remotely online.

A sample of our courses include:

- Managing Staff Remotely
- Positive Mental Attitude P.M.A.
- Self-Esteem
- Train the Trainer
- Confidence
- Coaching Skills
- Management Skills
- Leadership Skills
- Mental Health First Aid
- Interview Preparation

Contact us at info@targettrg.co.uk

Our customers love us!
⭐ Trustpilot

www.targettrg.co.uk or www.targettrg.com

JCRM Publishing   target
training associates

www.targettrg.co.uk

Published in 2020 by JCRM Publishing, UK

Designed and Produced by Ralph & Claire Moody

Copyright © JCRM Publishing & Target Training Associates 2020

This book is not intended to replace medical advice or treatment.

ISBN: 9798634764993

Positive Journal: Change your life with reflection and action. Available from Amazon and other leading retail outlets.

www.targettrg.co.uk

Retail enquiries to:
info@targettrg.co.uk

Positive
Journal

A journal for you to use and grow

RALPH & CLAIRE MOODY

JCRM Publishing

t**a**rget
training associates

www.targettrg.co.uk

POSITIVE JOURNAL

HOW TO USE THIS JOURNAL

A journal is a fantastic resource to write your thoughts every day. All you need to do is write for five minutes at the beginning of every day, or at the end of each day or both, it's your choice. Writing in a journal can create significant changes in your life when done correctly. We have both benefitted writing in a journal. It's an excellent opportunity to create a habit and build this into your life and make it part of your daily routine.

The purpose of this journal is to create positive thoughts. If you sit with just thinking you will think negatively, so the key is to create the pattern to write positively. If you force yourself to write positively, you will slowly change the way you think, increasing the success in your life. Don't make it a tick box exercise, so it becomes a chore, make it something you look forward to doing, writing your thoughts and feelings on paper so you can reflect and look back.

We have put together a 100 day journal with separate reflection sheets every ten days, one midway and then the final page. Reflection is essential when writing your journal to see what words keep jumping out. If you find yourself writing the same things recognise this, then think why am I doing this, am I stuck? This will help you think differently and look for other areas to think and feel. It may feel hard to write positively every day, that is good, you want that because change will be happening. You want to feel the uncomfortable feeling, that feeling will then become comfortable.

You will have a much more positive mindset on completion of this journal, and there is no doubt you will find yourself making improvements in your life. It is little changes that create change, positive change, that is if you decide to do this.

Writing a journal is a fantastic journey, good luck and enjoy the very special thoughts and moments you will create for yourself.

Enjoy!

Ralph & Claire

Claire and Ralph Moody

Ralph & Claire Moody
Founders of targettrg.co.uk

HOW TO USE THE JOURNAL

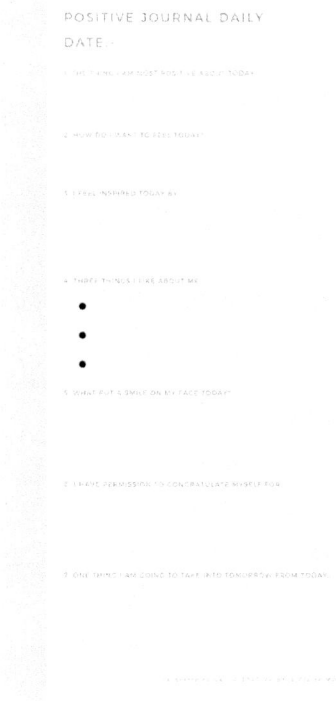

POSITIVE JOURNAL DAILY   DAY 1
DATE:-

The daily sheets are for you to complete in the morning or evening before you go to bed, it is up to you. Make sure you complete all questions.

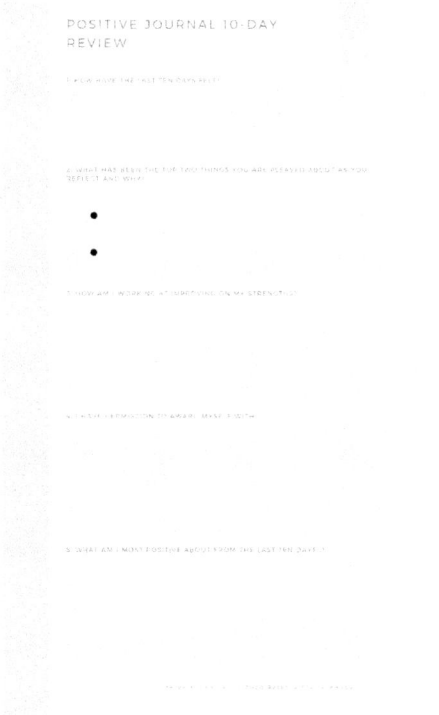

POSITIVE JOURNAL 10-DAY
REVIEW

Every 10 days complete a review of your actions and reflect on what you have achieved.

DATE:-

1: THE THING I AM MOST POSITIVE ABOUT TODAY?

2: HOW DO I WANT TO FEEL TODAY?

3: I FEEL INSPIRED TODAY BY...

4: THREE THINGS I LIKE ABOUT ME...

-
-
-

5: WHAT PUT A SMILE ON MY FACE TODAY?

6: I HAVE PERMISSION TO CONGRATULATE MYSELF FOR...

7: ONE THING I AM GOING TO TAKE INTO TOMORROW FROM TODAY...

DATE:-

1: THE THING I AM MOST POSITIVE ABOUT TODAY?

2: HOW DO I WANT TO FEEL TODAY?

3: I FEEL INSPIRED TODAY BY...

4: THREE THINGS I LIKE ABOUT ME...

-
-
-

5: WHAT PUT A SMILE ON MY FACE TODAY?

6: I HAVE PERMISSION TO CONGRATULATE MYSELF FOR...

7: ONE THING I AM GOING TO TAKE INTO TOMORROW FROM TODAY...

DATE:-

1: THE THING I AM MOST POSITIVE ABOUT TODAY?

2: HOW DO I WANT TO FEEL TODAY?

3: I FEEL INSPIRED TODAY BY...

4: THREE THINGS I LIKE ABOUT ME...

-
-
-

5: WHAT PUT A SMILE ON MY FACE TODAY?

6: I HAVE PERMISSION TO CONGRATULATE MYSELF FOR...

7: ONE THING I AM GOING TO TAKE INTO TOMORROW FROM TODAY...

DATE:-

1: THE THING I AM MOST POSITIVE ABOUT TODAY?

2: HOW DO I WANT TO FEEL TODAY?

3: I FEEL INSPIRED TODAY BY...

4: THREE THINGS I LIKE ABOUT ME...

-
-
-

5: WHAT PUT A SMILE ON MY FACE TODAY?

6: I HAVE PERMISSION TO CONGRATULATE MYSELF FOR...

7: ONE THING I AM GOING TO TAKE INTO TOMORROW FROM TODAY...

DATE:-

1: THE THING I AM MOST POSITIVE ABOUT TODAY?

2: HOW DO I WANT TO FEEL TODAY?

3: I FEEL INSPIRED TODAY BY...

4: THREE THINGS I LIKE ABOUT ME...

-
-
-

5: WHAT PUT A SMILE ON MY FACE TODAY?

6: I HAVE PERMISSION TO CONGRATULATE MYSELF FOR...

7: ONE THING I AM GOING TO TAKE INTO TOMORROW FROM TODAY...

DATE:-

1: THE THING I AM MOST POSITIVE ABOUT TODAY?

2: HOW DO I WANT TO FEEL TODAY?

3: I FEEL INSPIRED TODAY BY...

4: THREE THINGS I LIKE ABOUT ME...

-
-
-

5: WHAT PUT A SMILE ON MY FACE TODAY?

6: I HAVE PERMISSION TO CONGRATULATE MYSELF FOR...

7: ONE THING I AM GOING TO TAKE INTO TOMORROW FROM TODAY...

DATE:-

1: THE THING I AM MOST POSITIVE ABOUT TODAY?

2: HOW DO I WANT TO FEEL TODAY?

3: I FEEL INSPIRED TODAY BY...

4: THREE THINGS I LIKE ABOUT ME...

-
-
-

5: WHAT PUT A SMILE ON MY FACE TODAY?

6: I HAVE PERMISSION TO CONGRATULATE MYSELF FOR...

7: ONE THING I AM GOING TO TAKE INTO TOMORROW FROM TODAY...

DATE:-

1: THE THING I AM MOST POSITIVE ABOUT TODAY?

2: HOW DO I WANT TO FEEL TODAY?

3: I FEEL INSPIRED TODAY BY...

4: THREE THINGS I LIKE ABOUT ME...

-
-
-

5: WHAT PUT A SMILE ON MY FACE TODAY?

6: I HAVE PERMISSION TO CONGRATULATE MYSELF FOR...

7: ONE THING I AM GOING TO TAKE INTO TOMORROW FROM TODAY...

DATE:-

1: THE THING I AM MOST POSITIVE ABOUT TODAY?

2: HOW DO I WANT TO FEEL TODAY?

3: I FEEL INSPIRED TODAY BY...

4: THREE THINGS I LIKE ABOUT ME...

-
-
-

5: WHAT PUT A SMILE ON MY FACE TODAY?

6: I HAVE PERMISSION TO CONGRATULATE MYSELF FOR...

7: ONE THING I AM GOING TO TAKE INTO TOMORROW FROM TODAY...

DATE:-

1: THE THING I AM MOST POSITIVE ABOUT TODAY?

2: HOW DO I WANT TO FEEL TODAY?

3: I FEEL INSPIRED TODAY BY...

4: THREE THINGS I LIKE ABOUT ME...

-
-
-

5: WHAT PUT A SMILE ON MY FACE TODAY?

6: I HAVE PERMISSION TO CONGRATULATE MYSELF FOR...

7: ONE THING I AM GOING TO TAKE INTO TOMORROW FROM TODAY...

POSITIVE JOURNAL DAY 10 REVIEW

1: HOW HAVE THE LAST TEN DAYS FELT?

2: WHAT HAS BEEN THE TOP TWO THINGS YOU ARE PLEASED ABOUT AS YOU REFLECT AND WHY?

-
-

3: HOW AM I WORKING AT IMPROVING ON MY STRENGTHS?

4: I HAVE PERMISSION TO AWARD MYSELF WITH….

5: WHAT AM I MOST POSITIVE ABOUT FROM THE LAST TEN DAYS…?

DATE:-

1: THE THING I AM MOST POSITIVE ABOUT TODAY?

2: HOW DO I WANT TO FEEL TODAY?

3: I FEEL INSPIRED TODAY BY...

4: THREE THINGS I LIKE ABOUT ME...

-
-
-

5: WHAT PUT A SMILE ON MY FACE TODAY?

6: I HAVE PERMISSION TO CONGRATULATE MYSELF FOR...

7: ONE THING I AM GOING TO TAKE INTO TOMORROW FROM TODAY...

DATE:-

1: THE THING I AM MOST POSITIVE ABOUT TODAY?

2: HOW DO I WANT TO FEEL TODAY?

3: I FEEL INSPIRED TODAY BY...

4: THREE THINGS I LIKE ABOUT ME...

-
-
-

5: WHAT PUT A SMILE ON MY FACE TODAY?

6: I HAVE PERMISSION TO CONGRATULATE MYSELF FOR...

7: ONE THING I AM GOING TO TAKE INTO TOMORROW FROM TODAY...

DATE:-

1: THE THING I AM MOST POSITIVE ABOUT TODAY?

2: HOW DO I WANT TO FEEL TODAY?

3: I FEEL INSPIRED TODAY BY...

4: THREE THINGS I LIKE ABOUT ME...

-
-
-

5: WHAT PUT A SMILE ON MY FACE TODAY?

6: I HAVE PERMISSION TO CONGRATULATE MYSELF FOR...

7: ONE THING I AM GOING TO TAKE INTO TOMORROW FROM TODAY...

DATE:-

1: THE THING I AM MOST POSITIVE ABOUT TODAY?

2: HOW DO I WANT TO FEEL TODAY?

3: I FEEL INSPIRED TODAY BY...

4: THREE THINGS I LIKE ABOUT ME...

-
-
-

5: WHAT PUT A SMILE ON MY FACE TODAY?

6: I HAVE PERMISSION TO CONGRATULATE MYSELF FOR...

7: ONE THING I AM GOING TO TAKE INTO TOMORROW FROM TODAY...

DATE:-

1: THE THING I AM MOST POSITIVE ABOUT TODAY?

2: HOW DO I WANT TO FEEL TODAY?

3: I FEEL INSPIRED TODAY BY...

4: THREE THINGS I LIKE ABOUT ME...

-
-
-

5: WHAT PUT A SMILE ON MY FACE TODAY?

6: I HAVE PERMISSION TO CONGRATULATE MYSELF FOR...

7: ONE THING I AM GOING TO TAKE INTO TOMORROW FROM TODAY...

DATE:-

1: THE THING I AM MOST POSITIVE ABOUT TODAY?

2: HOW DO I WANT TO FEEL TODAY?

3: I FEEL INSPIRED TODAY BY...

4: THREE THINGS I LIKE ABOUT ME...

-
-
-

5: WHAT PUT A SMILE ON MY FACE TODAY?

6: I HAVE PERMISSION TO CONGRATULATE MYSELF FOR...

7: ONE THING I AM GOING TO TAKE INTO TOMORROW FROM TODAY...

DATE:-

1: THE THING I AM MOST POSITIVE ABOUT TODAY?

2: HOW DO I WANT TO FEEL TODAY?

3: I FEEL INSPIRED TODAY BY...

4: THREE THINGS I LIKE ABOUT ME...

-
-
-

5: WHAT PUT A SMILE ON MY FACE TODAY?

6: I HAVE PERMISSION TO CONGRATULATE MYSELF FOR...

7: ONE THING I AM GOING TO TAKE INTO TOMORROW FROM TODAY...

DATE:-

1: THE THING I AM MOST POSITIVE ABOUT TODAY?

2: HOW DO I WANT TO FEEL TODAY?

3: I FEEL INSPIRED TODAY BY...

4: THREE THINGS I LIKE ABOUT ME...

-
-
-

5: WHAT PUT A SMILE ON MY FACE TODAY?

6: I HAVE PERMISSION TO CONGRATULATE MYSELF FOR...

7: ONE THING I AM GOING TO TAKE INTO TOMORROW FROM TODAY...

DATE:-

1: THE THING I AM MOST POSITIVE ABOUT TODAY?

2: HOW DO I WANT TO FEEL TODAY?

3: I FEEL INSPIRED TODAY BY...

4: THREE THINGS I LIKE ABOUT ME...

-
-
-

5: WHAT PUT A SMILE ON MY FACE TODAY?

6: I HAVE PERMISSION TO CONGRATULATE MYSELF FOR...

7: ONE THING I AM GOING TO TAKE INTO TOMORROW FROM TODAY...

DATE:-

1: THE THING I AM MOST POSITIVE ABOUT TODAY?

2: HOW DO I WANT TO FEEL TODAY?

3: I FEEL INSPIRED TODAY BY...

4: THREE THINGS I LIKE ABOUT ME...

-
-
-

5: WHAT PUT A SMILE ON MY FACE TODAY?

6: I HAVE PERMISSION TO CONGRATULATE MYSELF FOR...

7: ONE THING I AM GOING TO TAKE INTO TOMORROW FROM TODAY...

POSITIVE JOURNAL DAY 20 REVIEW

1: HOW HAVE THE LAST TEN DAYS FELT?

2: WHAT HAS BEEN THE TOP TWO THINGS YOU ARE PLEASED ABOUT AS YOU REFLECT AND WHY?

-
-

3: HOW AM I WORKING AT IMPROVING ON MY STRENGTHS?

4: I HAVE PERMISSION TO AWARD MYSELF WITH….

5: WHAT AM I MOST POSITIVE ABOUT FROM THE LAST TEN DAYS…?

DATE:-

1: THE THING I AM MOST POSITIVE ABOUT TODAY?

2: HOW DO I WANT TO FEEL TODAY?

3: I FEEL INSPIRED TODAY BY...

4: THREE THINGS I LIKE ABOUT ME...

-
-
-

5: WHAT PUT A SMILE ON MY FACE TODAY?

6: I HAVE PERMISSION TO CONGRATULATE MYSELF FOR...

7: ONE THING I AM GOING TO TAKE INTO TOMORROW FROM TODAY...

DATE:-

1: THE THING I AM MOST POSITIVE ABOUT TODAY?

2: HOW DO I WANT TO FEEL TODAY?

3: I FEEL INSPIRED TODAY BY...

4: THREE THINGS I LIKE ABOUT ME...

-
-
-

5: WHAT PUT A SMILE ON MY FACE TODAY?

6: I HAVE PERMISSION TO CONGRATULATE MYSELF FOR...

7: ONE THING I AM GOING TO TAKE INTO TOMORROW FROM TODAY...

DATE:-

1: THE THING I AM MOST POSITIVE ABOUT TODAY?

2: HOW DO I WANT TO FEEL TODAY?

3: I FEEL INSPIRED TODAY BY...

4: THREE THINGS I LIKE ABOUT ME...

-
-
-

5: WHAT PUT A SMILE ON MY FACE TODAY?

6: I HAVE PERMISSION TO CONGRATULATE MYSELF FOR...

7: ONE THING I AM GOING TO TAKE INTO TOMORROW FROM TODAY...

DATE:-

1: THE THING I AM MOST POSITIVE ABOUT TODAY?

2: HOW DO I WANT TO FEEL TODAY?

3: I FEEL INSPIRED TODAY BY...

4: THREE THINGS I LIKE ABOUT ME...

-
-
-

5: WHAT PUT A SMILE ON MY FACE TODAY?

6: I HAVE PERMISSION TO CONGRATULATE MYSELF FOR...

7: ONE THING I AM GOING TO TAKE INTO TOMORROW FROM TODAY...

DATE:-

1: THE THING I AM MOST POSITIVE ABOUT TODAY?

2: HOW DO I WANT TO FEEL TODAY?

3: I FEEL INSPIRED TODAY BY...

4: THREE THINGS I LIKE ABOUT ME...

-
-
-

5: WHAT PUT A SMILE ON MY FACE TODAY?

6: I HAVE PERMISSION TO CONGRATULATE MYSELF FOR...

7: ONE THING I AM GOING TO TAKE INTO TOMORROW FROM TODAY...

DATE:-

1: THE THING I AM MOST POSITIVE ABOUT TODAY?

2: HOW DO I WANT TO FEEL TODAY?

3: I FEEL INSPIRED TODAY BY...

4: THREE THINGS I LIKE ABOUT ME...

-
-
-

5: WHAT PUT A SMILE ON MY FACE TODAY?

6: I HAVE PERMISSION TO CONGRATULATE MYSELF FOR...

7: ONE THING I AM GOING TO TAKE INTO TOMORROW FROM TODAY...

DATE:-

1: THE THING I AM MOST POSITIVE ABOUT TODAY?

2: HOW DO I WANT TO FEEL TODAY?

3: I FEEL INSPIRED TODAY BY...

4: THREE THINGS I LIKE ABOUT ME...

-
-
-

5: WHAT PUT A SMILE ON MY FACE TODAY?

6: I HAVE PERMISSION TO CONGRATULATE MYSELF FOR...

7: ONE THING I AM GOING TO TAKE INTO TOMORROW FROM TODAY...

DATE:-

1: THE THING I AM MOST POSITIVE ABOUT TODAY?

2: HOW DO I WANT TO FEEL TODAY?

3: I FEEL INSPIRED TODAY BY...

4: THREE THINGS I LIKE ABOUT ME...

-
-
-

5: WHAT PUT A SMILE ON MY FACE TODAY?

6: I HAVE PERMISSION TO CONGRATULATE MYSELF FOR...

7: ONE THING I AM GOING TO TAKE INTO TOMORROW FROM TODAY...

DATE:-

1: THE THING I AM MOST POSITIVE ABOUT TODAY?

2: HOW DO I WANT TO FEEL TODAY?

3: I FEEL INSPIRED TODAY BY...

4: THREE THINGS I LIKE ABOUT ME...

-
-
-

5: WHAT PUT A SMILE ON MY FACE TODAY?

6: I HAVE PERMISSION TO CONGRATULATE MYSELF FOR...

7: ONE THING I AM GOING TO TAKE INTO TOMORROW FROM TODAY...

DATE:-

1: THE THING I AM MOST POSITIVE ABOUT TODAY?

2: HOW DO I WANT TO FEEL TODAY?

3: I FEEL INSPIRED TODAY BY...

4: THREE THINGS I LIKE ABOUT ME...

-
-
-

5: WHAT PUT A SMILE ON MY FACE TODAY?

6: I HAVE PERMISSION TO CONGRATULATE MYSELF FOR...

7: ONE THING I AM GOING TO TAKE INTO TOMORROW FROM TODAY...

POSITIVE JOURNAL DAY 30 REVIEW

1: HOW HAVE THE LAST TEN DAYS FELT?

2: WHAT HAS BEEN THE TOP TWO THINGS YOU ARE PLEASED ABOUT AS YOU REFLECT AND WHY?

-
-

3: HOW AM I WORKING AT IMPROVING ON MY STRENGTHS?

4: I HAVE PERMISSION TO AWARD MYSELF WITH….

5: WHAT AM I MOST POSITIVE ABOUT FROM THE LAST TEN DAYS…?

DATE:-

1: THE THING I AM MOST POSITIVE ABOUT TODAY?

2: HOW DO I WANT TO FEEL TODAY?

3: I FEEL INSPIRED TODAY BY...

4: THREE THINGS I LIKE ABOUT ME...

-
-
-

5: WHAT PUT A SMILE ON MY FACE TODAY?

6: I HAVE PERMISSION TO CONGRATULATE MYSELF FOR...

7: ONE THING I AM GOING TO TAKE INTO TOMORROW FROM TODAY...

DATE:-

1: THE THING I AM MOST POSITIVE ABOUT TODAY?

2: HOW DO I WANT TO FEEL TODAY?

3: I FEEL INSPIRED TODAY BY...

4: THREE THINGS I LIKE ABOUT ME...

-
-
-

5: WHAT PUT A SMILE ON MY FACE TODAY?

6: I HAVE PERMISSION TO CONGRATULATE MYSELF FOR...

7: ONE THING I AM GOING TO TAKE INTO TOMORROW FROM TODAY...

DATE:-

1: THE THING I AM MOST POSITIVE ABOUT TODAY?

2: HOW DO I WANT TO FEEL TODAY?

3: I FEEL INSPIRED TODAY BY...

4: THREE THINGS I LIKE ABOUT ME...

-
-
-

5: WHAT PUT A SMILE ON MY FACE TODAY?

6: I HAVE PERMISSION TO CONGRATULATE MYSELF FOR...

7: ONE THING I AM GOING TO TAKE INTO TOMORROW FROM TODAY...

DATE:-

1: THE THING I AM MOST POSITIVE ABOUT TODAY?

2: HOW DO I WANT TO FEEL TODAY?

3: I FEEL INSPIRED TODAY BY...

4: THREE THINGS I LIKE ABOUT ME...

-
-
-

5: WHAT PUT A SMILE ON MY FACE TODAY?

6: I HAVE PERMISSION TO CONGRATULATE MYSELF FOR...

7: ONE THING I AM GOING TO TAKE INTO TOMORROW FROM TODAY...

DATE:-

1: THE THING I AM MOST POSITIVE ABOUT TODAY?

2: HOW DO I WANT TO FEEL TODAY?

3: I FEEL INSPIRED TODAY BY...

4: THREE THINGS I LIKE ABOUT ME...

-
-
-

5: WHAT PUT A SMILE ON MY FACE TODAY?

6: I HAVE PERMISSION TO CONGRATULATE MYSELF FOR...

7: ONE THING I AM GOING TO TAKE INTO TOMORROW FROM TODAY...

DATE:-

1: THE THING I AM MOST POSITIVE ABOUT TODAY?

2: HOW DO I WANT TO FEEL TODAY?

3: I FEEL INSPIRED TODAY BY...

4: THREE THINGS I LIKE ABOUT ME...

-
-
-

5: WHAT PUT A SMILE ON MY FACE TODAY?

6: I HAVE PERMISSION TO CONGRATULATE MYSELF FOR...

7: ONE THING I AM GOING TO TAKE INTO TOMORROW FROM TODAY...

DATE:-

1: THE THING I AM MOST POSITIVE ABOUT TODAY?

2: HOW DO I WANT TO FEEL TODAY?

3: I FEEL INSPIRED TODAY BY...

4: THREE THINGS I LIKE ABOUT ME...

-
-
-

5: WHAT PUT A SMILE ON MY FACE TODAY?

6: I HAVE PERMISSION TO CONGRATULATE MYSELF FOR...

7: ONE THING I AM GOING TO TAKE INTO TOMORROW FROM TODAY...

DATE:-

1: THE THING I AM MOST POSITIVE ABOUT TODAY?

2: HOW DO I WANT TO FEEL TODAY?

3: I FEEL INSPIRED TODAY BY...

4: THREE THINGS I LIKE ABOUT ME...

-
-
-

5: WHAT PUT A SMILE ON MY FACE TODAY?

6: I HAVE PERMISSION TO CONGRATULATE MYSELF FOR...

7: ONE THING I AM GOING TO TAKE INTO TOMORROW FROM TODAY...

DATE:-

1: THE THING I AM MOST POSITIVE ABOUT TODAY?

2: HOW DO I WANT TO FEEL TODAY?

3: I FEEL INSPIRED TODAY BY...

4: THREE THINGS I LIKE ABOUT ME...

-
-
-

5: WHAT PUT A SMILE ON MY FACE TODAY?

6: I HAVE PERMISSION TO CONGRATULATE MYSELF FOR...

7: ONE THING I AM GOING TO TAKE INTO TOMORROW FROM TODAY...

DATE:-

1: THE THING I AM MOST POSITIVE ABOUT TODAY?

2: HOW DO I WANT TO FEEL TODAY?

3: I FEEL INSPIRED TODAY BY...

4: THREE THINGS I LIKE ABOUT ME...

-
-
-

5: WHAT PUT A SMILE ON MY FACE TODAY?

6: I HAVE PERMISSION TO CONGRATULATE MYSELF FOR...

7: ONE THING I AM GOING TO TAKE INTO TOMORROW FROM TODAY...

POSITIVE JOURNAL DAY 40 REVIEW

1: HOW HAVE THE LAST TEN DAYS FELT?

2: WHAT HAS BEEN THE TOP TWO THINGS YOU ARE PLEASED ABOUT AS YOU REFLECT AND WHY?

-
-

3: HOW AM I WORKING AT IMPROVING ON MY STRENGTHS?

4: I HAVE PERMISSION TO AWARD MYSELF WITH....

5: WHAT AM I MOST POSITIVE ABOUT FROM THE LAST TEN DAYS...?

DATE:-

1: THE THING I AM MOST POSITIVE ABOUT TODAY?

2: HOW DO I WANT TO FEEL TODAY?

3: I FEEL INSPIRED TODAY BY...

4: THREE THINGS I LIKE ABOUT ME...

-
-
-

5: WHAT PUT A SMILE ON MY FACE TODAY?

6: I HAVE PERMISSION TO CONGRATULATE MYSELF FOR...

7: ONE THING I AM GOING TO TAKE INTO TOMORROW FROM TODAY...

DATE:-

1: THE THING I AM MOST POSITIVE ABOUT TODAY?

2: HOW DO I WANT TO FEEL TODAY?

3: I FEEL INSPIRED TODAY BY...

4: THREE THINGS I LIKE ABOUT ME...

-
-
-

5: WHAT PUT A SMILE ON MY FACE TODAY?

6: I HAVE PERMISSION TO CONGRATULATE MYSELF FOR...

7: ONE THING I AM GOING TO TAKE INTO TOMORROW FROM TODAY...

DATE:-

1: THE THING I AM MOST POSITIVE ABOUT TODAY?

2: HOW DO I WANT TO FEEL TODAY?

3: I FEEL INSPIRED TODAY BY...

4: THREE THINGS I LIKE ABOUT ME...

-
-
-

5: WHAT PUT A SMILE ON MY FACE TODAY?

6: I HAVE PERMISSION TO CONGRATULATE MYSELF FOR...

7: ONE THING I AM GOING TO TAKE INTO TOMORROW FROM TODAY...

DATE:-

1: THE THING I AM MOST POSITIVE ABOUT TODAY?

2: HOW DO I WANT TO FEEL TODAY?

3: I FEEL INSPIRED TODAY BY...

4: THREE THINGS I LIKE ABOUT ME...

-
-
-

5: WHAT PUT A SMILE ON MY FACE TODAY?

6: I HAVE PERMISSION TO CONGRATULATE MYSELF FOR...

7: ONE THING I AM GOING TO TAKE INTO TOMORROW FROM TODAY...

DATE:-

1: THE THING I AM MOST POSITIVE ABOUT TODAY?

2: HOW DO I WANT TO FEEL TODAY?

3: I FEEL INSPIRED TODAY BY...

4: THREE THINGS I LIKE ABOUT ME...

-
-
-

5: WHAT PUT A SMILE ON MY FACE TODAY?

6: I HAVE PERMISSION TO CONGRATULATE MYSELF FOR...

7: ONE THING I AM GOING TO TAKE INTO TOMORROW FROM TODAY...

DATE:-

1: THE THING I AM MOST POSITIVE ABOUT TODAY?

2: HOW DO I WANT TO FEEL TODAY?

3: I FEEL INSPIRED TODAY BY...

4: THREE THINGS I LIKE ABOUT ME...

-
-
-

5: WHAT PUT A SMILE ON MY FACE TODAY?

6: I HAVE PERMISSION TO CONGRATULATE MYSELF FOR...

7: ONE THING I AM GOING TO TAKE INTO TOMORROW FROM TODAY...

DATE:-

1: THE THING I AM MOST POSITIVE ABOUT TODAY?

2: HOW DO I WANT TO FEEL TODAY?

3: I FEEL INSPIRED TODAY BY...

4: THREE THINGS I LIKE ABOUT ME...

-
-
-

5: WHAT PUT A SMILE ON MY FACE TODAY?

6: I HAVE PERMISSION TO CONGRATULATE MYSELF FOR...

7: ONE THING I AM GOING TO TAKE INTO TOMORROW FROM TODAY...

POSITIVE JOURNAL DAILY

DATE:-

1: THE THING I AM MOST POSITIVE ABOUT TODAY?

2: HOW DO I WANT TO FEEL TODAY?

3: I FEEL INSPIRED TODAY BY...

4: THREE THINGS I LIKE ABOUT ME...

-
-
-

5: WHAT PUT A SMILE ON MY FACE TODAY?

6: I HAVE PERMISSION TO CONGRATULATE MYSELF FOR...

7: ONE THING I AM GOING TO TAKE INTO TOMORROW FROM TODAY...

DATE:-

1: THE THING I AM MOST POSITIVE ABOUT TODAY?

2: HOW DO I WANT TO FEEL TODAY?

3: I FEEL INSPIRED TODAY BY...

4: THREE THINGS I LIKE ABOUT ME...

-
-
-

5: WHAT PUT A SMILE ON MY FACE TODAY?

6: I HAVE PERMISSION TO CONGRATULATE MYSELF FOR...

7: ONE THING I AM GOING TO TAKE INTO TOMORROW FROM TODAY...

DATE:-

1: THE THING I AM MOST POSITIVE ABOUT TODAY?

2: HOW DO I WANT TO FEEL TODAY?

3: I FEEL INSPIRED TODAY BY...

4: THREE THINGS I LIKE ABOUT ME...

-
-
-

5: WHAT PUT A SMILE ON MY FACE TODAY?

6: I HAVE PERMISSION TO CONGRATULATE MYSELF FOR...

7: ONE THING I AM GOING TO TAKE INTO TOMORROW FROM TODAY...

POSITIVE JOURNAL DAY 50 REVIEW

1: HOW HAVE THE LAST TEN DAYS FELT?

2: WHAT HAS BEEN THE TOP TWO THINGS YOU ARE PLEASED ABOUT AS YOU REFLECT AND WHY?

-
-

3: HOW AM I WORKING AT IMPROVING ON MY STRENGTHS?

4: I HAVE PERMISSION TO AWARD MYSELF WITH….

5: WHAT AM I MOST POSITIVE ABOUT FROM THE LAST TEN DAYS…?

Day 50
Congratulations

Congratulations for meeting the halfway point, tremendous effort and fantastic that you are growing in positivity. The book is for you only, very personnel and as you reflect on the last fifty days, look at your incredible journey. Every little change is the change you need to move forward. Think about achieving your goal of increased positivity, what will it feel like at day 100, just imagine that feeling.

DATE:-

1: THE THING I AM MOST POSITIVE ABOUT TODAY?

2: HOW DO I WANT TO FEEL TODAY?

3: I FEEL INSPIRED TODAY BY...

4: THREE THINGS I LIKE ABOUT ME...

-
-
-

5: WHAT PUT A SMILE ON MY FACE TODAY?

6: I HAVE PERMISSION TO CONGRATULATE MYSELF FOR...

7: ONE THING I AM GOING TO TAKE INTO TOMORROW FROM TODAY...

DATE:-

1: THE THING I AM MOST POSITIVE ABOUT TODAY?

2: HOW DO I WANT TO FEEL TODAY?

3: I FEEL INSPIRED TODAY BY...

4: THREE THINGS I LIKE ABOUT ME...

-
-
-

5: WHAT PUT A SMILE ON MY FACE TODAY?

6: I HAVE PERMISSION TO CONGRATULATE MYSELF FOR...

7: ONE THING I AM GOING TO TAKE INTO TOMORROW FROM TODAY...

DATE:-

1: THE THING I AM MOST POSITIVE ABOUT TODAY?

2: HOW DO I WANT TO FEEL TODAY?

3: I FEEL INSPIRED TODAY BY...

4: THREE THINGS I LIKE ABOUT ME...

-
-
-

5: WHAT PUT A SMILE ON MY FACE TODAY?

6: I HAVE PERMISSION TO CONGRATULATE MYSELF FOR...

7: ONE THING I AM GOING TO TAKE INTO TOMORROW FROM TODAY...

DATE:-

1: THE THING I AM MOST POSITIVE ABOUT TODAY?

2: HOW DO I WANT TO FEEL TODAY?

3: I FEEL INSPIRED TODAY BY...

4: THREE THINGS I LIKE ABOUT ME...

-
-
-

5: WHAT PUT A SMILE ON MY FACE TODAY?

6: I HAVE PERMISSION TO CONGRATULATE MYSELF FOR...

7: ONE THING I AM GOING TO TAKE INTO TOMORROW FROM TODAY...

DATE:-

1: THE THING I AM MOST POSITIVE ABOUT TODAY?

2: HOW DO I WANT TO FEEL TODAY?

3: I FEEL INSPIRED TODAY BY...

4: THREE THINGS I LIKE ABOUT ME...

-
-
-

5: WHAT PUT A SMILE ON MY FACE TODAY?

6: I HAVE PERMISSION TO CONGRATULATE MYSELF FOR...

7: ONE THING I AM GOING TO TAKE INTO TOMORROW FROM TODAY...

DATE:-

1: THE THING I AM MOST POSITIVE ABOUT TODAY?

2: HOW DO I WANT TO FEEL TODAY?

3: I FEEL INSPIRED TODAY BY...

4: THREE THINGS I LIKE ABOUT ME...

-
-
-

5: WHAT PUT A SMILE ON MY FACE TODAY?

6: I HAVE PERMISSION TO CONGRATULATE MYSELF FOR...

7: ONE THING I AM GOING TO TAKE INTO TOMORROW FROM TODAY...

DATE:-

1: THE THING I AM MOST POSITIVE ABOUT TODAY?

2: HOW DO I WANT TO FEEL TODAY?

3: I FEEL INSPIRED TODAY BY...

4: THREE THINGS I LIKE ABOUT ME...

-
-
-

5: WHAT PUT A SMILE ON MY FACE TODAY?

6: I HAVE PERMISSION TO CONGRATULATE MYSELF FOR...

7: ONE THING I AM GOING TO TAKE INTO TOMORROW FROM TODAY...

DATE:-

1: THE THING I AM MOST POSITIVE ABOUT TODAY?

2: HOW DO I WANT TO FEEL TODAY?

3: I FEEL INSPIRED TODAY BY...

4: THREE THINGS I LIKE ABOUT ME...

-
-
-

5: WHAT PUT A SMILE ON MY FACE TODAY?

6: I HAVE PERMISSION TO CONGRATULATE MYSELF FOR...

7: ONE THING I AM GOING TO TAKE INTO TOMORROW FROM TODAY...

DATE:-

1: THE THING I AM MOST POSITIVE ABOUT TODAY?

2: HOW DO I WANT TO FEEL TODAY?

3: I FEEL INSPIRED TODAY BY...

4: THREE THINGS I LIKE ABOUT ME...

-
-
-

5: WHAT PUT A SMILE ON MY FACE TODAY?

6: I HAVE PERMISSION TO CONGRATULATE MYSELF FOR...

7: ONE THING I AM GOING TO TAKE INTO TOMORROW FROM TODAY...

DATE:-

1: THE THING I AM MOST POSITIVE ABOUT TODAY?

2: HOW DO I WANT TO FEEL TODAY?

3: I FEEL INSPIRED TODAY BY...

4: THREE THINGS I LIKE ABOUT ME...

-
-
-

5: WHAT PUT A SMILE ON MY FACE TODAY?

6: I HAVE PERMISSION TO CONGRATULATE MYSELF FOR...

7: ONE THING I AM GOING TO TAKE INTO TOMORROW FROM TODAY...

POSITIVE JOURNAL DAY 60 REVIEW

1: HOW HAVE THE LAST TEN DAYS FELT?

2: WHAT HAS BEEN THE TOP TWO THINGS YOU ARE PLEASED ABOUT AS YOU REFLECT AND WHY?

-
-

3: HOW AM I WORKING AT IMPROVING ON MY STRENGTHS?

4: I HAVE PERMISSION TO AWARD MYSELF WITH....

5: WHAT AM I MOST POSITIVE ABOUT FROM THE LAST TEN DAYS...?

DATE:-

1: THE THING I AM MOST POSITIVE ABOUT TODAY?

2: HOW DO I WANT TO FEEL TODAY?

3: I FEEL INSPIRED TODAY BY...

4: THREE THINGS I LIKE ABOUT ME...

-
-
-

5: WHAT PUT A SMILE ON MY FACE TODAY?

6: I HAVE PERMISSION TO CONGRATULATE MYSELF FOR...

7: ONE THING I AM GOING TO TAKE INTO TOMORROW FROM TODAY...

DATE:-

1: THE THING I AM MOST POSITIVE ABOUT TODAY?

2: HOW DO I WANT TO FEEL TODAY?

3: I FEEL INSPIRED TODAY BY...

4: THREE THINGS I LIKE ABOUT ME...

-
-
-

5: WHAT PUT A SMILE ON MY FACE TODAY?

6: I HAVE PERMISSION TO CONGRATULATE MYSELF FOR...

7: ONE THING I AM GOING TO TAKE INTO TOMORROW FROM TODAY...

DATE:-

1: THE THING I AM MOST POSITIVE ABOUT TODAY?

2: HOW DO I WANT TO FEEL TODAY?

3: I FEEL INSPIRED TODAY BY...

4: THREE THINGS I LIKE ABOUT ME...

-
-
-

5: WHAT PUT A SMILE ON MY FACE TODAY?

6: I HAVE PERMISSION TO CONGRATULATE MYSELF FOR...

7: ONE THING I AM GOING TO TAKE INTO TOMORROW FROM TODAY...

DATE:-

1: THE THING I AM MOST POSITIVE ABOUT TODAY?

2: HOW DO I WANT TO FEEL TODAY?

3: I FEEL INSPIRED TODAY BY...

4: THREE THINGS I LIKE ABOUT ME...

-
-
-

5: WHAT PUT A SMILE ON MY FACE TODAY?

6: I HAVE PERMISSION TO CONGRATULATE MYSELF FOR...

7: ONE THING I AM GOING TO TAKE INTO TOMORROW FROM TODAY...

DATE:-

1: THE THING I AM MOST POSITIVE ABOUT TODAY?

2: HOW DO I WANT TO FEEL TODAY?

3: I FEEL INSPIRED TODAY BY...

4: THREE THINGS I LIKE ABOUT ME...

-
-
-

5: WHAT PUT A SMILE ON MY FACE TODAY?

6: I HAVE PERMISSION TO CONGRATULATE MYSELF FOR...

7: ONE THING I AM GOING TO TAKE INTO TOMORROW FROM TODAY...

DATE:-

1: THE THING I AM MOST POSITIVE ABOUT TODAY?

2: HOW DO I WANT TO FEEL TODAY?

3: I FEEL INSPIRED TODAY BY...

4: THREE THINGS I LIKE ABOUT ME...

-
-
-

5: WHAT PUT A SMILE ON MY FACE TODAY?

6: I HAVE PERMISSION TO CONGRATULATE MYSELF FOR...

7: ONE THING I AM GOING TO TAKE INTO TOMORROW FROM TODAY...

DATE:-

1: THE THING I AM MOST POSITIVE ABOUT TODAY?

2: HOW DO I WANT TO FEEL TODAY?

3: I FEEL INSPIRED TODAY BY...

4: THREE THINGS I LIKE ABOUT ME...

-
-
-

5: WHAT PUT A SMILE ON MY FACE TODAY?

6: I HAVE PERMISSION TO CONGRATULATE MYSELF FOR...

7: ONE THING I AM GOING TO TAKE INTO TOMORROW FROM TODAY...

DATE:-

1: THE THING I AM MOST POSITIVE ABOUT TODAY?

2: HOW DO I WANT TO FEEL TODAY?

3: I FEEL INSPIRED TODAY BY...

4: THREE THINGS I LIKE ABOUT ME...

-
-
-

5: WHAT PUT A SMILE ON MY FACE TODAY?

6: I HAVE PERMISSION TO CONGRATULATE MYSELF FOR...

7: ONE THING I AM GOING TO TAKE INTO TOMORROW FROM TODAY...

DATE:-

1: THE THING I AM MOST POSITIVE ABOUT TODAY?

2: HOW DO I WANT TO FEEL TODAY?

3: I FEEL INSPIRED TODAY BY...

4: THREE THINGS I LIKE ABOUT ME...

-
-
-

5: WHAT PUT A SMILE ON MY FACE TODAY?

6: I HAVE PERMISSION TO CONGRATULATE MYSELF FOR...

7: ONE THING I AM GOING TO TAKE INTO TOMORROW FROM TODAY...

DATE:-

1: THE THING I AM MOST POSITIVE ABOUT TODAY?

2: HOW DO I WANT TO FEEL TODAY?

3: I FEEL INSPIRED TODAY BY...

4: THREE THINGS I LIKE ABOUT ME...

-
-
-

5: WHAT PUT A SMILE ON MY FACE TODAY?

6: I HAVE PERMISSION TO CONGRATULATE MYSELF FOR...

7: ONE THING I AM GOING TO TAKE INTO TOMORROW FROM TODAY...

POSITIVE JOURNAL DAY 70 REVIEW

1: HOW HAVE THE LAST TEN DAYS FELT?

2: WHAT HAS BEEN THE TOP TWO THINGS YOU ARE PLEASED ABOUT AS YOU REFLECT AND WHY?

-
-

3: HOW AM I WORKING AT IMPROVING ON MY STRENGTHS?

4: I HAVE PERMISSION TO AWARD MYSELF WITH....

5: WHAT AM I MOST POSITIVE ABOUT FROM THE LAST TEN DAYS...?

DATE:-

1: THE THING I AM MOST POSITIVE ABOUT TODAY?

2: HOW DO I WANT TO FEEL TODAY?

3: I FEEL INSPIRED TODAY BY...

4: THREE THINGS I LIKE ABOUT ME...

-
-
-

5: WHAT PUT A SMILE ON MY FACE TODAY?

6: I HAVE PERMISSION TO CONGRATULATE MYSELF FOR...

7: ONE THING I AM GOING TO TAKE INTO TOMORROW FROM TODAY...

DATE:-

1: THE THING I AM MOST POSITIVE ABOUT TODAY?

2: HOW DO I WANT TO FEEL TODAY?

3: I FEEL INSPIRED TODAY BY...

4: THREE THINGS I LIKE ABOUT ME...

-
-
-

5: WHAT PUT A SMILE ON MY FACE TODAY?

6: I HAVE PERMISSION TO CONGRATULATE MYSELF FOR...

7: ONE THING I AM GOING TO TAKE INTO TOMORROW FROM TODAY...

DATE:-

1: THE THING I AM MOST POSITIVE ABOUT TODAY?

2: HOW DO I WANT TO FEEL TODAY?

3: I FEEL INSPIRED TODAY BY...

4: THREE THINGS I LIKE ABOUT ME...

-
-
-

5: WHAT PUT A SMILE ON MY FACE TODAY?

6: I HAVE PERMISSION TO CONGRATULATE MYSELF FOR...

7: ONE THING I AM GOING TO TAKE INTO TOMORROW FROM TODAY...

DATE:-

1: THE THING I AM MOST POSITIVE ABOUT TODAY?

2: HOW DO I WANT TO FEEL TODAY?

3: I FEEL INSPIRED TODAY BY...

4: THREE THINGS I LIKE ABOUT ME...

-
-
-

5: WHAT PUT A SMILE ON MY FACE TODAY?

6: I HAVE PERMISSION TO CONGRATULATE MYSELF FOR...

7: ONE THING I AM GOING TO TAKE INTO TOMORROW FROM TODAY...

DATE:-

1: THE THING I AM MOST POSITIVE ABOUT TODAY?

2: HOW DO I WANT TO FEEL TODAY?

3: I FEEL INSPIRED TODAY BY...

4: THREE THINGS I LIKE ABOUT ME...

-
-
-

5: WHAT PUT A SMILE ON MY FACE TODAY?

6: I HAVE PERMISSION TO CONGRATULATE MYSELF FOR...

7: ONE THING I AM GOING TO TAKE INTO TOMORROW FROM TODAY...

DATE:-

1: THE THING I AM MOST POSITIVE ABOUT TODAY?

2: HOW DO I WANT TO FEEL TODAY?

3: I FEEL INSPIRED TODAY BY...

4: THREE THINGS I LIKE ABOUT ME...

-
-
-

5: WHAT PUT A SMILE ON MY FACE TODAY?

6: I HAVE PERMISSION TO CONGRATULATE MYSELF FOR...

7: ONE THING I AM GOING TO TAKE INTO TOMORROW FROM TODAY...

DATE:-

1: THE THING I AM MOST POSITIVE ABOUT TODAY?

2: HOW DO I WANT TO FEEL TODAY?

3: I FEEL INSPIRED TODAY BY...

4: THREE THINGS I LIKE ABOUT ME...

-
-
-

5: WHAT PUT A SMILE ON MY FACE TODAY?

6: I HAVE PERMISSION TO CONGRATULATE MYSELF FOR...

7: ONE THING I AM GOING TO TAKE INTO TOMORROW FROM TODAY...

DATE:-

1: THE THING I AM MOST POSITIVE ABOUT TODAY?

2: HOW DO I WANT TO FEEL TODAY?

3: I FEEL INSPIRED TODAY BY...

4: THREE THINGS I LIKE ABOUT ME...

-
-
-

5: WHAT PUT A SMILE ON MY FACE TODAY?

6: I HAVE PERMISSION TO CONGRATULATE MYSELF FOR...

7: ONE THING I AM GOING TO TAKE INTO TOMORROW FROM TODAY...

POSITIVE JOURNAL DAILY   DAY 79

DATE:-

1: THE THING I AM MOST POSITIVE ABOUT TODAY?

2: HOW DO I WANT TO FEEL TODAY?

3: I FEEL INSPIRED TODAY BY...

4: THREE THINGS I LIKE ABOUT ME...

-
-
-

5: WHAT PUT A SMILE ON MY FACE TODAY?

6: I HAVE PERMISSION TO CONGRATULATE MYSELF FOR...

7: ONE THING I AM GOING TO TAKE INTO TOMORROW FROM TODAY...

DATE:-

1: THE THING I AM MOST POSITIVE ABOUT TODAY?

2: HOW DO I WANT TO FEEL TODAY?

3: I FEEL INSPIRED TODAY BY...

4: THREE THINGS I LIKE ABOUT ME...

-
-
-

5: WHAT PUT A SMILE ON MY FACE TODAY?

6: I HAVE PERMISSION TO CONGRATULATE MYSELF FOR...

7: ONE THING I AM GOING TO TAKE INTO TOMORROW FROM TODAY...

POSITIVE JOURNAL DAY 80 REVIEW

1: HOW HAVE THE LAST TEN DAYS FELT?

2: WHAT HAS BEEN THE TOP TWO THINGS YOU ARE PLEASED ABOUT AS YOU REFLECT AND WHY?

-
-

3: HOW AM I WORKING AT IMPROVING ON MY STRENGTHS?

4: I HAVE PERMISSION TO AWARD MYSELF WITH….

5: WHAT AM I MOST POSITIVE ABOUT FROM THE LAST TEN DAYS…?

DATE:-

1: THE THING I AM MOST POSITIVE ABOUT TODAY?

2: HOW DO I WANT TO FEEL TODAY?

3: I FEEL INSPIRED TODAY BY...

4: THREE THINGS I LIKE ABOUT ME...

-
-
-

5: WHAT PUT A SMILE ON MY FACE TODAY?

6: I HAVE PERMISSION TO CONGRATULATE MYSELF FOR...

7: ONE THING I AM GOING TO TAKE INTO TOMORROW FROM TODAY...

DATE:-

1: THE THING I AM MOST POSITIVE ABOUT TODAY?

2: HOW DO I WANT TO FEEL TODAY?

3: I FEEL INSPIRED TODAY BY...

4: THREE THINGS I LIKE ABOUT ME...

-
-
-

5: WHAT PUT A SMILE ON MY FACE TODAY?

6: I HAVE PERMISSION TO CONGRATULATE MYSELF FOR...

7: ONE THING I AM GOING TO TAKE INTO TOMORROW FROM TODAY...

DATE:-

1: THE THING I AM MOST POSITIVE ABOUT TODAY?

2: HOW DO I WANT TO FEEL TODAY?

3: I FEEL INSPIRED TODAY BY...

4: THREE THINGS I LIKE ABOUT ME...

-
-
-

5: WHAT PUT A SMILE ON MY FACE TODAY?

6: I HAVE PERMISSION TO CONGRATULATE MYSELF FOR...

7: ONE THING I AM GOING TO TAKE INTO TOMORROW FROM TODAY...

DATE:-

1: THE THING I AM MOST POSITIVE ABOUT TODAY?

2: HOW DO I WANT TO FEEL TODAY?

3: I FEEL INSPIRED TODAY BY...

4: THREE THINGS I LIKE ABOUT ME...

-
-
-

5: WHAT PUT A SMILE ON MY FACE TODAY?

6: I HAVE PERMISSION TO CONGRATULATE MYSELF FOR...

7: ONE THING I AM GOING TO TAKE INTO TOMORROW FROM TODAY...

DATE:-

1: THE THING I AM MOST POSITIVE ABOUT TODAY?

2: HOW DO I WANT TO FEEL TODAY?

3: I FEEL INSPIRED TODAY BY...

4: THREE THINGS I LIKE ABOUT ME...

-
-
-

5: WHAT PUT A SMILE ON MY FACE TODAY?

6: I HAVE PERMISSION TO CONGRATULATE MYSELF FOR...

7: ONE THING I AM GOING TO TAKE INTO TOMORROW FROM TODAY...

DATE:-

1: THE THING I AM MOST POSITIVE ABOUT TODAY?

2: HOW DO I WANT TO FEEL TODAY?

3: I FEEL INSPIRED TODAY BY...

4: THREE THINGS I LIKE ABOUT ME...

-
-
-

5: WHAT PUT A SMILE ON MY FACE TODAY?

6: I HAVE PERMISSION TO CONGRATULATE MYSELF FOR...

7: ONE THING I AM GOING TO TAKE INTO TOMORROW FROM TODAY...

DATE:-

1: THE THING I AM MOST POSITIVE ABOUT TODAY?

2: HOW DO I WANT TO FEEL TODAY?

3: I FEEL INSPIRED TODAY BY...

4: THREE THINGS I LIKE ABOUT ME...

-
-
-

5: WHAT PUT A SMILE ON MY FACE TODAY?

6: I HAVE PERMISSION TO CONGRATULATE MYSELF FOR...

7: ONE THING I AM GOING TO TAKE INTO TOMORROW FROM TODAY...

POSITIVE JOURNAL DAILY

DATE:-

1: THE THING I AM MOST POSITIVE ABOUT TODAY?

2: HOW DO I WANT TO FEEL TODAY?

3: I FEEL INSPIRED TODAY BY...

4: THREE THINGS I LIKE ABOUT ME...

-
-
-

5: WHAT PUT A SMILE ON MY FACE TODAY?

6: I HAVE PERMISSION TO CONGRATULATE MYSELF FOR...

7: ONE THING I AM GOING TO TAKE INTO TOMORROW FROM TODAY...

DATE:-

1: THE THING I AM MOST POSITIVE ABOUT TODAY?

2: HOW DO I WANT TO FEEL TODAY?

3: I FEEL INSPIRED TODAY BY...

4: THREE THINGS I LIKE ABOUT ME...

-
-
-

5: WHAT PUT A SMILE ON MY FACE TODAY?

6: I HAVE PERMISSION TO CONGRATULATE MYSELF FOR...

7: ONE THING I AM GOING TO TAKE INTO TOMORROW FROM TODAY...

DATE:-

1: THE THING I AM MOST POSITIVE ABOUT TODAY?

2: HOW DO I WANT TO FEEL TODAY?

3: I FEEL INSPIRED TODAY BY...

4: THREE THINGS I LIKE ABOUT ME...

-
-
-

5: WHAT PUT A SMILE ON MY FACE TODAY?

6: I HAVE PERMISSION TO CONGRATULATE MYSELF FOR...

7: ONE THING I AM GOING TO TAKE INTO TOMORROW FROM TODAY...

POSITIVE JOURNAL DAY 90 REVIEW

1: HOW HAVE THE LAST TEN DAYS FELT?

2: WHAT HAS BEEN THE TOP TWO THINGS YOU ARE PLEASED ABOUT AS YOU REFLECT AND WHY?

-
-

3: HOW AM I WORKING AT IMPROVING ON MY STRENGTHS?

4: I HAVE PERMISSION TO AWARD MYSELF WITH....

5: WHAT AM I MOST POSITIVE ABOUT FROM THE LAST TEN DAYS...?

POSITIVE JOURNAL DAILY DAY 91

DATE:-

1: THE THING I AM MOST POSITIVE ABOUT TODAY?

2: HOW DO I WANT TO FEEL TODAY?

3: I FEEL INSPIRED TODAY BY...

4: THREE THINGS I LIKE ABOUT ME...

-
-
-

5: WHAT PUT A SMILE ON MY FACE TODAY?

6: I HAVE PERMISSION TO CONGRATULATE MYSELF FOR...

7: ONE THING I AM GOING TO TAKE INTO TOMORROW FROM TODAY...

DATE:-

1: THE THING I AM MOST POSITIVE ABOUT TODAY?

2: HOW DO I WANT TO FEEL TODAY?

3: I FEEL INSPIRED TODAY BY...

4: THREE THINGS I LIKE ABOUT ME...

-
-
-

5: WHAT PUT A SMILE ON MY FACE TODAY?

6: I HAVE PERMISSION TO CONGRATULATE MYSELF FOR...

7: ONE THING I AM GOING TO TAKE INTO TOMORROW FROM TODAY...

DATE:-

1: THE THING I AM MOST POSITIVE ABOUT TODAY?

2: HOW DO I WANT TO FEEL TODAY?

3: I FEEL INSPIRED TODAY BY...

4: THREE THINGS I LIKE ABOUT ME...

-
-
-

5: WHAT PUT A SMILE ON MY FACE TODAY?

6: I HAVE PERMISSION TO CONGRATULATE MYSELF FOR...

7: ONE THING I AM GOING TO TAKE INTO TOMORROW FROM TODAY...

DATE:-

1: THE THING I AM MOST POSITIVE ABOUT TODAY?

2: HOW DO I WANT TO FEEL TODAY?

3: I FEEL INSPIRED TODAY BY...

4: THREE THINGS I LIKE ABOUT ME...

-
-
-

5: WHAT PUT A SMILE ON MY FACE TODAY?

6: I HAVE PERMISSION TO CONGRATULATE MYSELF FOR...

7: ONE THING I AM GOING TO TAKE INTO TOMORROW FROM TODAY...

DATE:-

1: THE THING I AM MOST POSITIVE ABOUT TODAY?

2: HOW DO I WANT TO FEEL TODAY?

3: I FEEL INSPIRED TODAY BY...

4: THREE THINGS I LIKE ABOUT ME...

-
-
-

5: WHAT PUT A SMILE ON MY FACE TODAY?

6: I HAVE PERMISSION TO CONGRATULATE MYSELF FOR...

7: ONE THING I AM GOING TO TAKE INTO TOMORROW FROM TODAY...

DATE:-

1: THE THING I AM MOST POSITIVE ABOUT TODAY?

2: HOW DO I WANT TO FEEL TODAY?

3: I FEEL INSPIRED TODAY BY...

4: THREE THINGS I LIKE ABOUT ME...

-
-
-

5: WHAT PUT A SMILE ON MY FACE TODAY?

6: I HAVE PERMISSION TO CONGRATULATE MYSELF FOR...

7: ONE THING I AM GOING TO TAKE INTO TOMORROW FROM TODAY...

DATE:-

1: THE THING I AM MOST POSITIVE ABOUT TODAY?

2: HOW DO I WANT TO FEEL TODAY?

3: I FEEL INSPIRED TODAY BY...

4: THREE THINGS I LIKE ABOUT ME...

-
-
-

5: WHAT PUT A SMILE ON MY FACE TODAY?

6: I HAVE PERMISSION TO CONGRATULATE MYSELF FOR...

7: ONE THING I AM GOING TO TAKE INTO TOMORROW FROM TODAY...

DATE:-

1: THE THING I AM MOST POSITIVE ABOUT TODAY?

2: HOW DO I WANT TO FEEL TODAY?

3: I FEEL INSPIRED TODAY BY...

4: THREE THINGS I LIKE ABOUT ME...

-
-
-

5: WHAT PUT A SMILE ON MY FACE TODAY?

6: I HAVE PERMISSION TO CONGRATULATE MYSELF FOR...

7: ONE THING I AM GOING TO TAKE INTO TOMORROW FROM TODAY...

DATE:-

1: THE THING I AM MOST POSITIVE ABOUT TODAY?

2: HOW DO I WANT TO FEEL TODAY?

3: I FEEL INSPIRED TODAY BY...

4: THREE THINGS I LIKE ABOUT ME...

-
-
-

5: WHAT PUT A SMILE ON MY FACE TODAY?

6: I HAVE PERMISSION TO CONGRATULATE MYSELF FOR...

7: ONE THING I AM GOING TO TAKE INTO TOMORROW FROM TODAY...

DATE:-

1: THE THING I AM MOST POSITIVE ABOUT TODAY?

2: HOW DO I WANT TO FEEL TODAY?

3: I FEEL INSPIRED TODAY BY...

4: THREE THINGS I LIKE ABOUT ME...

-
-
-

5: WHAT PUT A SMILE ON MY FACE TODAY?

6: I HAVE PERMISSION TO CONGRATULATE MYSELF FOR...

7: ONE THING I AM GOING TO TAKE INTO TOMORROW FROM TODAY...

POSITIVE JOURNAL DAY 100 REVIEW

1: HOW HAVE THE LAST TEN DAYS FELT?

2: WHAT HAS BEEN THE TOP TWO THINGS YOU ARE PLEASED ABOUT AS YOU REFLECT AND WHY?

-
-

3: HOW AM I WORKING AT IMPROVING ON MY STRENGTHS?

4: I HAVE PERMISSION TO AWARD MYSELF WITH....

5: WHAT AM I MOST POSITIVE ABOUT FROM THE LAST TEN DAYS...?

Day 100
Congratulations

Congratulations on achieving 100 days of positive thoughts. You have completed and reflected on your strengths and now have a better understanding of your real positive self. You have our permission to give yourself an award for achieving this fantastic milestone. Now think about how you can take this forward and grow further, amazing stuff.

POSITIVE JOURNAL
MEET THE AUTHORS

JCRM Publishing

t**rget
training associates

www.targettrg.co.uk

RALPH MOODY

Ralph believes that lifelong learning is precisely that, and should not be limited by age or perceived ability. He has a belief that all of us have the potential to do anything if we put our minds to it. Armed with the right skills, knowledge and attitude, we can all perform to the highest standards. Moreover, his philosophy is that limiting belief is what holds the majority of people back and that, with appropriate coaching, mentoring and training, we can all achieve anything. With over 30 years of training experience, he specialises in trainer, management and leadership development.

> *"Life is a gift and we all have a responsibility to make the most of it, so that when we look back, we know it wasn't wasted"*
>
> RALPH MOODY

CLAIRE MOODY

Claire is an extremely experienced trainer and coach at Target Training, and you can always guarantee she will deliver outstanding results: she is incredibly passionate about both her training and coaching. She has over 35 years' experience in training, coaching and quality assurance roles, with experience as a teacher and in Train the Trainer, working with international clients. Moreover, she has expertise in the management of trainer inductions, standardisation and quality assurance for corporate clients. She holds an MSc in executive coaching and is accredited by Ashridge, a world leader in executive coach training and development. Additionally, she specialises in psychometric assessment, including MBTI.

> *"It's not about being the best, it's about being the best you can be"*
>
> CLAIRE MOODY

HAVE QUESTIONS?

Target Training Associates
107 Cheapside, London, EC2V 6DN
0800 302 9344
info@targettrg.co.uk
www.targettrg.co.uk

SOME OTHER TITLES IN THE JOURNAL SERIES

Daily Journal
Thank You Journal
Growing Confidence Journal
Improve Self Esteem Journal
Fitness Journal
Rainbow Food Journal
Action Planning Journal
Time Management Journal
Management Journal

Made in the USA
Las Vegas, NV
06 December 2021